Original title:
Berries on the Wind

Author: Miriam Kensington
ISBN HARDBACK: 978-1-80586-414-1
ISBN PAPERBACK: 978-1-80586-886-6

Ambrosia of the Wild Places

In the breeze, a dance they twirl,
A splash of color, a joyful swirl.
Red hats on green, oh what a sight,
Nature's jesters in pure delight.

They giggle like kids in the sun,
Rolling and tumbling, oh what fun!
Plump little orbs with laughter to share,
Tickling the leaves in the warm spring air.

A pluck, a squish, a playful mess,
Juicy secrets in this wilderness.
Wobbling together, they bounce and hop,
A fruity parade that never will stop.

So let us join in this silly spree,
With nature's confetti, wild and free.
Under the canopy, we'll dance and spin,
In the wild places, where giggles begin.

The Overture of Subtle Colors

Fluffy clouds with a wink and a nudge,
While tiny fruits dance in a light-heartedudge.
They chortle and tickle with vibrant cheer,
A carnival feel, oh, what a dear!

Orange and purple, they mingle and clash,
Atop little stalks, they bounce and thrash.
Each plump little friend with a tale to tell,
As they wiggle and jiggle, you can’t help but dwell.

Like fruity jesters, they prank and tease,
Blowing soft kisses with the softest breeze.
They wear crowns of dew in a sparkling crown,
Come join the fun, don’t be a clown!

So take a stroll where the colors collide,
And let the laughter be your guide.
In this cheerful realm, you’ll find a spark,
As nature’s palette ignites the dark.

Lush Vibrations in the Green

In the garden, giggles grow,
Chasing critters to and fro.
Berry stains on cheeks so bright,
A fruity brawl, what a sight!

Juicy drops, a tasty fight,
Rolling laughter, pure delight.
Silly hats upon our heads,
As we dance on leafy beds!

Starlit Rhapsody of Fruit

Under stars, we gather round,
With strange fruits from the ground.
Tasting colors, oh what fun,
Joking 'bout each stylish pun.

Glittering skins and wobbly shapes,
Unlikely pals, these funny drapes.
With each bite, a silly face,
Giggles bounce from place to place.

Rippling Flavors on Nature's Canvas

Splash of red, a twist of sweet,
Smudged on noses, sticky feet.
Creamy clouds of whipped adorn,
Every berry dance is born.

Taste of laughter fills the air,
Each creation a wild affair.
Painting smiles on summer's cheek,
Tickled tongues with laughter speak!

Gentle Hues of Harvest Time

When harvest moon begins to rise,
Fruits parade in silly guise.
Purple hats and orange ties,
Nature's joke beneath the skies!

Chuckling squirrels with nutty plans,
Pirates sought with berry cans.
A treasure chest of fruity cheer,
Harvest giggles shared, oh dear!

Aromas Swirling through the Fields

In the field where giggles bloom,
Fragrant whispers chase the gloom.
Old man Jim with a wobbly hat,
Says the flowers are chatting, fancy that!

Butterflies laugh, they twirl and spin,
In a dance where grins begin.
They nibble on petals, try a bite,
While ants march by, a comical sight.

Pastels Floating on Gentle Currents

Pink clouds drift like cotton candy,
A squirrel dips nuts, oh so dandy!
With a splash of cream, they float on by,
The wind tickles, making all sigh.

Frogs croak out silly serenades,
As shades of laughter fill the glades.
A duck quacks jokes, winking an eye,
And even the shy bloom can't help but sigh.

Gatherings of Nature's Gifts

Gather round the merry crowd,
Nature's treasures, all sing loud.
Mice with hats, a wild affair,
Party when the sun's in the air!

Giggling bees buzz sweetly near,
Each buzz a note, so full of cheer.
They dance with joy, no time to spare,
As petals sway, none can compare.

Tufts of Flavor in the Breeze

Puffs of flavor, oh what a tease,
Float through air with such great ease.
A hedgehog speaks of fruity dreams,
While sipping tea from little streams.

The wind blows tales of taste and cheer,
As creatures gather, all appear.
In a swirl of giggles and surprises,
Nature’s feast brings many disguises.

Serenade of Summer's Hues

Glistening gems in a bright blue sky,
Fruits take flight, oh me, oh my!
A plump raspberry, with a grin so wide,
Tumbles down, what a joyous ride!

Lemon drops dance like they own the day,
Tickling noses, 'Hey, come out and play!'
With each twist and turn, laughter rings clear,
As giggles mingle in the warm summer sphere.

Wild Fruits in Flight

Strawberries giggle while swirling around,
Dodging the bees, they leap from the ground!
A blueberry winks, with a cheeky jest,
'Take a deep breath, forget all the rest!'

Raspberry rascals on a merry old spree,
Paint the sky wild, come laugh with me!
They bounce through the air, sprightly and spry,
Chasing clouds like they're flying pie!

A Breath of Red and Blue

Dancing in clusters, oh what a sight,
Tiny treats twirl in the morning light.
A cherry chimes with a sing-song tone,
While little grapes play, never alone!

Blue jiggly pals in a jubilant race,
Chase the wind's laughter, oh what a place!
'Catch us if you can!' they all shout in glee,
As we skip together, wild and free.

Nature's Juicy Secrets

A sneaky peach whispers cheekily low,
'Come closer now, shh, don’t you know?'
In the rustle of leaves, secrets unfold,
Mischievous flavors, daring and bold!

Plum pranks abound, with a wink and a toss,
Hiding in bushes, they’re never at a loss.
Each juicy secret brings laughter and cheer,
Unraveling joys as the season draws near.

Nature's Palette in Motion

In the field, colors dance and sway,
A snack parade, come join the fray.
Tiny globes in hues so bright,
Who knew munching could be such a delight?

Tiny critters buzz with glee,
Gobbled up, oh what a spree!
Nature's art, a fun buffet,
What else can we grab today?

Sweet Ribbons of Flora

Tangled vines and joyful sights,
A feast of laughter, pure delights.
Sticky fingers, oh what fun,
Let's play tag, then bask in the sun!

Colors twirl like kids at play,
Whispers tickle, come what may.
In this garden, all's a race,
Munch and giggle, embrace the chase!

Lush Cascades of Color

Rolling hills of vibrant glee,
Tiptoes through vitality.
A little pluck, a shiny treat,
Nature's candy, oh so sweet!

Bumbles laugh with every bite,
Gourmet joy, what a sight!
Ticklish breeze, let’s all spin,
Chasing flavors on a whim!

The Hum of Flavorful Whispers

A buzzing tune fills the air,
Nature's gossip everywhere.
Chatter leads to a fun chase,
Tickling toes in this wild space!

Juicy tales and silly cheer,
Join the feast, the fun is near!
Giggling leaves in playful brawl,
Come on folks, it's a free-for-all!

Garden Paths of Silken Sweets

In the garden where laughter sways,
Chasing critters on sunny days.
The strawberries giggle, bouncing around,
While raspberries dance without a sound.

A squirrel steals snacks, what a cheeky thief,
Sprinkling chaos like a comic relief.
The tomatoes blush, they're feeling shy,
While cucumbers roll, oh my, oh my!

The blueberries claim the top of the tree,
Holding court, as proud as can be.
Lemons are laughing, not wanting a fight,
Dancing with joy in the warm sunlight.

Oh, lemon meringue, what a silly twist,
Cakes and pies that no one can resist.
At the garden’s end, they all take a bow,
Life’s a feast, and they’re the stars, somehow!

Tapestry of Earth and Sun

A patchwork quilt of colors bright,
Sunshine tickles, oh what a sight!
Peas and carrots play tag in rows,
While the garlic whispers jokes nobody knows.

Pumpkins chuckle, their pouts all fake,
Rolling ‘round like a big birthday cake.
The cinnamon blasts a wafting cheer,
As rhubarb sings, ‘Come join us here!’

Fungi in hats, they throw a parade,
While ants in tuxes hustle and wade.
Flowers in hats, with feathers so grand,
Raise a toast with soil in their hand!

Every sprout has a tale to share,
As wind takes heed and ruffles their hair.
In this garden, the laughter’s a must,
Where dirt and dreams combine, and combust!

Radiance in a Rustic Cornucopia

In a basket bright with nature’s delight,
Veggies and fruits dance through the night.
Oranges giggle, their peels like confetti,
As carrots wiggle, all bouncy and ready.

Jams in jars are planning a show,
The pickles are prancing, like 'look at us go!'
Honeybees buzz with a tune in their flight,
Trading their nectar for a taste of the night.

Potatoes grumble, ‘Just wait, we’ll surprise!’
While radishes pop out with sparkling eyes.
A playful parade of flavors so grand,
Holding hands like children, all linked in a band.

In this bounty, fun times never end,
As each quirky fruit finds a new friend.
Life’s a banquet, partake with a grin,
Dance with your veggies, let the feast begin!

Celestial Fragments at Dawn

Stars have winked, the sky starts to laugh,
Morning's bright face, a cheeky giraffe.
Bluejays chime with a hooty song,
While sleepy dew drops tag along.

Sunlight spills like a clumsy spill,
Cakes and pastries are trying to chill.
Twinkling doughnuts roll off the shelf,
While cookies whisper, 'We need some help!'

Moonbeams dance in a wild prance,
Exploring flavors, oh what a chance!
Bananas play peek-a-boo with the light,
As pancakes flip, preparing for flight.

In this light-hearted, sweet panorama,
Honey drips down like a funny drama.
So sip your milk and chuckle with me,
At this breakfast bash, pure glee is the key!

A Drift of Orchard Echoes

In the orchard, laughter flies,
Chasing fruit beneath blue skies.
A squirrel steals a juicy snack,
As giggles bounce and echoes clack.

A tumble here, a stumble there,
Nature's glee is in the air.
With sticky fingers, kids delight,
And jam-filled dreams take off in flight.

Savoring Nature's Sweet Remembrances

A picnic spread with color bold,
Grandma's stories never old.
With raspberry juice on my chin,
Life's humorous, where to begin?

A blueberry fight breaks out with glee,
Sticky smiles, you and me.
As we laugh and dodge the stains,
Mother Nature's sweet refrains.

The Pulse of Fruiting Vines

Grapes hang low, tempt fate's embrace,
With each pluck, we engage in race.
A friend trips, the fruit flies high,
Whirling through the bright blue sky.

In a game of fruity dodgeball,
Laughter crescendos, where's the fall?
With every bounce, we feel alive,
Harvest joy on which we thrive.

Tasting the Season's Breath

Come gather 'round for a fruity feast,
Where flavors clash like wild beasts.
Watermelon wars, juicy delight,
Splashes of fun in the fading light.

Strawberry tales of summer’s yore,
As hidden giggles bloom and soar.
With every bite, we dance and twirl,
In a berry blissful whirl.

The Rustle of Flora's Blessings

In the garden, a dance begins,
With tiny fruits and silly grins.
Their laughter spills on summer's breath,
As petals giggle, teasing death.

A squirrel wears a berry crown,
As bees buzz by, spinning round.
The sun peeks in, a cheeky flirt,
While fruits plop down, red and pert.

A rabbit hops, all full of sass,
As juicy gifts fall from the grass.
The sky above is bright and clear,
While nature's jokes bring endless cheer.

Oh, Flora's gifts, a merry sight,
With nature’s jesters taking flight.
With every rustle, joy unwinds,
And sunshine tickles silly minds.

Puffs of Color through the Air

A splash of red, a dash of hue,
A berry ball rolls past my shoe.
It giggles and hops, avoiding me,
With chubby cheeks, it flies so free.

A pie's been stolen, oh dear fate,
The crust left crisp, a little late.
The thief grins wide, a berry bandit,
And laughs out loud, oh how he planned it.

The flowers wink, they know the score,
As fruit-filled puffs come tumbling more.
A purple one zips by my ear,
And in the chaos, all's good cheer.

With color splashed upon the ground,
The world is full of fruit profound.
A playful breeze decides its art,
As fruity laughter warms the heart.

Whispers of Wild Harvest

In the woods where secrets play,
Fruits plot mischief every day.
They scheme with leaves to catch a breeze,
In wild whispers, with such ease.

A blueberry winks and takes a dive,
While a cheeky cherry starts to jive.
They twirl and spin in nature’s ball,
And giggle softly with it all.

Nuts join in, with courage stout,
As citrus fellows start to shout.
Together they dance, a comical scene,
As laughter blooms, so bright and keen.

In the harvest's embrace, joy unfolds,
With every berry, a tale retold.
Oh, wild whispers float to the sky,
Where fruity dreams forever fly.

Fruits Skimming the Horizon

Far off where the blueberry waves,
The horizon laughs and misbehaves.
With fruit so bold, they take their flight,
And sing their songs through day and night.

A peach takes off on a gusty ride,
With plums that cheer while spinning wide.
They race the clouds, oh what a scene,
With giggles echoing, bright and keen.

The apples tumble, a wild show,
Rolling down from hills of glow.
They tease the breeze, and dance along,
Creating rhythms, fruity song.

At sunset, the laughter starts to fade,
As fruits return, their games well-played.
With dreams of skimming, they take a bow,
In the dusk's embrace, they're silent now.

Gliding on Hidden Currents

A squirrel in a top hat leaps,
Chasing dreams that the gust keeps.
With acorns spinning, he twirls late,
Laughs at himself, back at his fate.

Leaves dance while he wobbles near,
The jesters of the forest cheer.
A feather floats, he tips his cup,
With every stumble, he won't give up.

Whimsical winds weave tales on high,
His tiny feet, they leap and fly.
Each twist in the air spins a tale,
Where giggles linger, never stale.

The breeze carries whispers of glee,
His mighty jump, a sight to see.
In the playful swirl of leafy green,
Life's just a jolly, silly routine.

Harvested Echoes of Lost Days

An old banana's in the spotlight,
Crowned with laughter, feeling just right.
“Once I was ripe, now look at me!”
Sings to strawberries with glee.

The jokes from oranges roll around,
Each punchline bounces off the ground.
“Remember when we were all so sweet?”
Now we parade, a slightly gray fleet.

The past holds punchlines we all shared,
In jars of jam, dreams declared.
Each squished grape has a fable to tell,
Of sunny days and slips as well.

Tasty whispers from the orchard roam,
In this merry land, we found our home.
With every chuckle, we shake our head,
In the harvest of laughter, we are fed.

Vignettes in Flavorful Flight

A robin hops, his beak a brush,
Painting the air in a vibrant rush.
Berry juice stains the path he leaves,
Tickling the roots of playful leaves.

A cheeky fox with a grape hat struts,
In a world of flavors, he giggles, oh guts!
Chasing after clouds made of cream,
A whimsical, frothy, fruit-filled dream.

The picnic ants bring bags of fun,
Pineapple hats for everyone!
They waddle and wiggle, a sight to see,
Their tiny dance, the world's jubilee!

As nature giggles, the fruits conspire,
To spread sweet warmth and laughter's fire.
In the air, the nectar drips bright,
Moments of joy take glamorous flight.

The Pulse of Nature's Melody

In the quiet grove, a tune takes shape,
The plum plays jazz, in a fruity cape.
While lemons twinkle in a tight ballet,
And cherries giggle in a bright array.

A trumpet berry lets out a laugh,
Waves of rhythm, they dance and quaff.
The wind joins in with a high-pitched cheer,
Echoing laughter for all to hear.

Whimsical notes float through the trees,
A carrot joins in, strumming with ease.
Odd instruments from every berry tale,
In this orchestra, we shall not fail.

Nature’s pulse beats in soft delight,
As critters sway, the stars grow bright.
With every chuckle, the symphony plays,
A mashup of joy that never decays.

The Breath of Forest Delicacies

In the forest where giggles bloom,
Fruits tumble like whispers, with joy they zoom.
A squirrel's dance, a raccoon's laugh,
Nature's buffet, a sweet little gaffe.

Lemonade clouds float up high,
While the blueberries play peek-a-boo, oh my!
With each berry popping, a tickle's delight,
As sunlight sprinkles, they're ready for flight.

A strawberry slipped on a splashy scene,
Wiggles and jiggles, all getting keen.
Who knew the woods could chuckle and cheer?
With laughter and sweetness, they always appear.

Pine cones tease, and the daisies prance,
In this fruity frolic, everyone's a chance.
So weave in the whimsy, let joy be your friend,
In the breath of luscious, the fun never ends.

Vibrant Words from Sugary Chords

On a vine of laughter, the tales unwind,
Strawberries nodding, oh what a find!
The raspberries whisper in mischievous tunes,
Tickling the air where fun gently croons.

Tangerine dreams roll down the lane,
While giggles pop like champagne in the rain.
Bananas join in with a comical swing,
As the forest chortles, life's a sweet fling.

Cherry cheeks blush in the lovely breeze,
Joking with sunlight, they dance through the trees.
Grapes do a tango, twirling in the sun,
Spreading out stories, they're never outdone.

Nature's symphony, vibrant and bold,
Plays with flavors, tales delightfully told.
Sweetness envelops, as laughter resounds,
In sugary chords where the joy never drowns.

Whispered Secrets of the Fruit-Laden Trees

Underneath the branches, secrets unfold,
A fig tells a story, oh, how it's bold!
Peaches giggle, rolling with glee,
While apples chuckle as they swing free.

Lemons plotting mischief with zestful intent,
While oranges holler, their energy spent.
A crow comes by, with a jest on his mind,
In this fruity ruckus, fun's one of a kind.

The trees whisper softly, with secrets that rise,
The fruits share a laugh, wrapped up in the skies.
Juicy confessions, ripe with pure cheer,
The forest, alive, making mischief sincere.

Days filled with joy, as colors all blend,
Hot sun on their skin, and laughter they send.
In the heart of the grove, let the raucous resound,
With whispered delight, in the beauty we've found.

Nature's Canvas of Shimmering Gems

Upon the canvas where colors collide,
Nature’s palette swirls, with humor inside.
A splash of blueberry, with giggles attached,
As cherry-red chuckles are quickly dispatched.

Violet slow dances on breezes so light,
While golden sunshine takes its joyful flight.
Fruits wearing crowns, prance madly around,
In this lively gallery, laughter is found.

Mangoes in ballerina skirts make a show,
While kiwi comes spinning, a fruit-shaped rodeo.
Pineapple jokes create a tropical scene,
As laughter erupts, painting the serene.

So come share the fun on this vibrant spree,
With nature as artist, wild and carefree.
In the shimmering gems, where whimsy ignites,
Let joy be your compass, and take to the heights.

The Flight of Juicy Echoes

Little seeds take to the sky,
They squabble as they flutter by.
One lands in a stranger's hat,
“Is that a berry? Or just a cat?”

Chasing each other with a cheer,
These fruity folks bring laughter near.
A tumble here, a giggle there,
What’s that? A grape just stole my chair!

Rolling along on a breeze so sweet,
They dance in patterns, skip and greet.
One slipped, a raspberry on the floor,
Knocking elbows, “Who ordered more?”

As they twist and turn in flight,
The ground below with sheer delight.
A plucky crew, they sing their song,
“Hey, join us here! You can’t go wrong!”

Petals in a Berry Breeze

Red and round, they laugh and roll,
Whisked away, they seek their goal.
One hollered "Hey, don't leave me here!"
The others danced, "Just shift your gear!"

Raspberries try to lead the pack,
While strawberries put on a whack!
A blueberry, bold, made a stand,
"I'll be king! This is my land!"

With a breeze that tickles and plays,
They swirl in whirlwinds, oh what a craze!
Petals giggle as they take flight,
A fruity fiesta, pure delight!

"Catch me if you can!" they sing,
A chase of sweetness, oh what a fling!
In a dance of joy, they twirl and spin,
In their world of fun, let the games begin!

Lullabies of Ripened Fruits

Beneath the sun, they gently sway,
A whispered song of a sunny day.
"My stem's a rocket, watch me zoom!"
As cherries giggle, making room.

They trade their tales of juicy pride,
With every nudge, a berry slide.
"Who wants a nap?" a plum declared,
But bouncing berries weren't prepared!

"Catch a ride on the dandelion's fluff!"
"Last one there must bring the stuff!"
The fruits fell over, in fits of glee,
Creating chaos - oh, the jubilee!

As twilight glows, lullabies weave,
"Goodnight, sweet friends, but don't you leave!"
They settle down, in a merry heap,
As stars above watch them safely sleep.

Chasing the Scent of Wildness

In a patch that glistens bright,
Berries zoom to the left and right.
“Catch my scent, oh come along!”
A zesty dance, wild and strong!

A tumble here, a splat over there,
They chase the dream without a care.
“Is that a grape or just my shoe?”
“No matter, let’s make a fruit stew!”

With laughter ringing through the air,
Berry friends let down their hair.
They leap and bound with giddy glee,
Chasing wildness, just wait and see!

And when the day draws to an end,
They share their jokes, as they descend.
With a wink, they whisper a plan,
“Tomorrow’s quest, let’s catch a fan!”

Tides of Woodland Temptations

A squirrel scowls at a berry treat,
Wondering why his prize is sweet.
He tosses it high, oh, what a tale!
It lands in a puddle, sailing like a whale.

The fox looks on with keen delight,
Sniffing the air, he's ready to bite.
But slippery berries shoot from his grasp,
He fumbles and tumbles with a laugh and a gasp.

The deer prances with a clumsy jig,
Chasing the drops like a playful pig.
They splatter and squirt, giggles ensue,
Who knew the forest was such a zoo?

In silence comes an old wise owl,
Who watches the chaos, raising a scowl.
With feathers fluffed and a haughty tone,
He hoots, "These fruits are best left alone!"

Sweetness in the Fragrant Air

A bumblebee buzzes with a wobbly grin,
Dancing around like a kid in a spin.
He lands on a berry, thinks it's a throne,
But slips off the edge, oh, how he has grown!

A rabbit roams with a curious nose,
Sniffing the sweetness no one else knows.
He dives for a treat; oh, what a sight!
Rolling and tumbling, what pure delight!

A gentle breeze, it carries a puff,
Of laughter and whispers, “Is that enough?”
The creatures all giggle at nature's own game,
Playing with flavors, they’ll never be tame!

The sun dips low, casting a glow,
On all the frolics in the fun below.
With every bounce and a playful cheer,
Who knew the forest could bring such a beer!

The Dance of Primordial Flavors

In the thicket nobody quite understands,
Fruits sing and giggle, they tease with hands.
A raccoon prances, thinking he's slick,
While blueberry plops land with a splish and a flick.

A chipmunk chuckles, packing a stash,
When a strawberry bounces and gives him a splash.
He laughs, "Oh dear, a berry's encore,"
As juicy rhythm leads him to the floor!

A lizard lurking, with eyes so wide,
Watches the madness he cannot abide.
He shimmies and shakes, joining the craze,
Who knew his day could end in a blaze?

With fruits all a-dancing, the air so sweet,
In a whimsical whirl, they clamor and greet.
While nature's flavors twist, flip, and swirl,
It's a berrylicious fun-filled world!

Nature's Colorful Serenade

A parrot squawks, with feathers bright,
Chasing the colors, a splendid sight.
He dives for a berry, turns green and blue,
Only to find he's stuck in a stew.

Meanwhile, a badger, oh what a sight,
Tries to do a jig in sheer delight.
With a berry stuck on the tip of his snout,
He wiggles and jiggles, with laughter about.

A hedgehog rolls, thinking it's all fair,
When a raspberry lands right in his hair.
With a giggle and squeak, he bursts into glee,
Crowned with fruit, oh who could disagree?

As twilight descends, colors clash and blend,
The forest's a playground, where fun has no end.
With chuckles and giggles, life's that grand show,
In this berry-filled frolic, let laughter flow!

Fleeting Flavors in the Twilight

A plump little berry, wearing a hat,
Said, "Watch my dance! I'm quite the acrobat!"
With a jig and a twirl, it rolled down the hill,
'Til it tripped on a leaf and said, "Oh, what a thrill!"

The sun chuckled softly, as shadows grew long,
While plumes of bright laughter sang sweet little songs.
As the dusk hit the stage, it changed all the rules,
Now the berries were hosting a party for fools!

With whispers of wishes, they painted the sky,
A sprinkle of magic made colors fly high.
The stars were the audience, clapping in cheer,
As the jamming red fruits made giggles appear!

So here's to the twilight and flavors so fun,
For a laughter-filled night has now just begun!
With a pop and a fizz, let the giggles pour in,
The party's just started—so let's spin again!

Chasing Drops of Summer Joy

In the field there was trouble, a one-man parade,
A raspberry yelled, "Don’t let me be swayed!"
With a hop and a skip, it dashed through the grass,
While the blueberries giggled, just watching it pass.

A strawberry strolled with a clumsy old grin,
Said, "I don't care if my leaves are all thin!"
"I’ll juggle some dew while exploring this place,
And prove that sweet fruits can keep up the pace!"

The bees buzzed their laughter, they joined in the chase,
As they twirled and they whirled in a juicy embrace.
Each drop was a blessing, each splash was a play,
Making summer feel brighter in every sweet way!

So let’s raise a toast to this fruity affair,
With laughter and joy, and a little sweet flair!
To the frolicsome moments that dance through the day,
As we chase every drop of summer away!

The Scent of Ruby Dreams

In a basket of dreams, where the colors collide,
A raspberry shouted, "I'm taking a ride!"
With sprinkles of joy and a pinch of delight,
It soared through the kitchen, the stars shining bright.

A blueberry fell flat, said, "What's all the fuss?
I'd rather be snacking than twirling in dust!"
But the others insisted, "You must join the show!
The aroma of bliss makes the best kind of glow!"

With laughter so sweet, they wove clouds of cheer,
Each nibble of flavor rang out loud and clear.
The jam-making symphony played on repeat,
As the fruits all convened for their big, fruity feat!

Let's dance through the night with our zesty delight,
For the scent of our dreams makes the world feel just right!
With a pop and a twist, let the flavors collide,
In this joyous adventure, let laughter be our guide!

When Nature's Treats Take Wing

One day a red currant, so bold and so spry,
Decided to run up and challenge the sky.
With a flap of its leaves, it leapt to the breeze,
"Catch me, my friends, if you dare—if you please!"

A cherry chimed in, "Well, I'm light as a feather,
I'll soar through the air, let's all fly together!"
With a giggle and whirl, they danced through the sun,
Claiming that flying was far more fun!

As they zipped through the garden, what a sight to behold,

These nature's sweet treats were both daring and bold!
A raspberry hiccupped, "Oh dear, I feel giddy,
Is it joy that I tasted, or something quite silly?"

So let's laugh with the fruits as they spin and they glide,
In a world where each harvest is one crazy ride.
When nature's sweet treasures decide to take flight,
You'll find giggles and joy, in the soft, twinkling night!

Tapestry of Nature's Offerings

In the garden, a riot of hues,
Each fruit with a laugh, each leaf with a muse.
A blueberry winks, a raspberry grins,
While strawberries bounce like they're in a spin.

Nature giggles in sun-soaked delight,
As squirrels dance underneath the moonlight.
With cheeky chews, they nibble with glee,
While the worms wriggle, sipping their tea.

The branches all sway, a whimsical tune,
Berries call out, making mischief at noon.
'Taste me, I dare you!' they squeal with a twist,
In this fruity frenzy, who could resist?

So gather your friends, and let laughter ring,
In the tapestry lush, where joy takes wing.
With nature's humor, let's frolic and play,
For every bright harvest brings smiles to our day.

Secrets Sung by the Wind

Listen closely to the whispers at dusk,
Secrets flutter by, in nature's bright husk.
A cheeky elderberry tells jokes with flair,
While a dandelion spins stories so rare.

As the breeze blows this tale of delight,
Blackberries chuckle, bursting in flight.
A raspberry once tried to take a small leap,
But landed in pie, a secret to keep!

Oh, the stories that nature would tell if it could,
Of errant cherries rolling in neighborhoods.
They'd laugh and they'd wiggle, a dance on the way,
As blueberries plot their grand jester play.

So join in the chorus, and sing with the trees,
Let laughter unfurl like petals in the breeze.
With nature's own secrets, let joy intertwine,
For those who seek humor will always find wine!

Kites of Crimson and Indigo

See the kites that dance in the sky,
Crimson and indigo, oh my, oh my!
Each puff of the wind sends them fluttering high,
Like cherries that giggle as they flit by.

They swoop and they swirl, no cares in the air,
As plump blackcurrants cause uproarious flair.
Each twist tells a tale of fruit-filled delight,
Where laughter springs free all through the night.

Grapes tumble down with a jiggly bounce,
Making the spectators giggle and pounce.
Fruits on the move, a hilarious spree,
As the whole world joins in this fruity jubilee!

So hoist up your kites, let joy take its stand,
With nibbles of nature, all fully planned.
For in colors so vivid, life finds a way,
To show us that laughter can brighten the day!

Petals and Fruit in Flight

Petals cascade, in a fragrant ballet,
Landing on berries as children at play.
A cantaloupe chuckles, and woofers all bark,
While musk melons giggle at larks in the park.

Each fruit takes a leap in a jolly parade,
Twirling and flipping in sunlight's cascade.
Bananas wear hats, and apples spin round,
While melons make music, a sweet, joyful sound.

The air is a canvas of color and cheer,
As fruits toss confetti, and laughter draws near.
With petals for pillows beneath all our feasts,
Nature's own antics bring smiles like an east!

So come join this revel, where sweetness is rife,
With petals and fruit, oh, the joy in this life.
Fluttering jokes as they lighten our load,
In this delightful realm, on a whimsical road.

Secrets Beneath the Rustling Leaves

In the bushes where giggles hide,
A squirrel danced with a berry pie.
He took a bite, it stained his face,
Now he runs a sticky race!

A robin joined, with flair and song,
Nibbled on treats, but something's wrong.
She chased her beak after a fly,
And ended up with jam on high!

The whispers of leaves, they chuckle near,
As ants parade, marching with cheer.
They've found a feast, a berry dome,
Now they're dragging treats back home!

Laughter echoes through the trees,
While critters plot their next big squeeze.
A picnic planned, no room for fright,
Just playful hearts and berry bites!

Flavors Carried by Gentle Currents

On a breeze, a sweet surprise,
Frogs croak jokes in slimy ties.
They hop about with such delight,
While ten tiny bugs hold their flight.

A duckling quacks, "This snack is grand!"
As cherries drift upon the sand.
He wobbles, splashes, makes a scene,
With berry juice, he's so obscene!

The river sings, a bubbly tune,
While fishes gasp, "A feast, we swoon!"
They dance through waves, oh what a show,
Berry cheeks aglow, they flow.

A turtle grins, slow yet sly,
Catching sweets that float on by.
Each splash a joke, each gulp a cheer,
Nature's laughter fills the sphere!

The Essence of Nature's Palette

Colors burst in nature’s scheme,
A painter’s laugh turns into cream.
Blue and red, so bright and bold,
With tasty tales yet to be told.

The sun dips low, it spills its gold,
While critters barter plots so old.
A raspberry belt, a berry race,
Who knew they had such style and grace?

Mice wear hats made of green leaves,
Debating if they should have peas.
With every munch, a fruity twist,
A feast so grand, none can resist!

While twilight brings a berry blush,
Creatures scatter, all in a rush.
In every nook, a laugh, a grin,
Nature’s palette, let the fun begin!

Clouded Paths of Berry Blossoms

Down the lane where giggles play,
A hedgehog hides, too shy today.
With berry hats and shoes so bright,
He peeks and ponders, what a sight!

Clouds above, they roll and sway,
While bees conduct their merry ballet.
"Buzz along," they cheer in rhyme,
"Who needs a tune when you've got thyme?"

A footrace starts, with critters squealed,
The prize? A pie, all berry-filled.
Each step a slip, in laughter's cheer,
As berry paths lead friends so near.

Through the drifts, a sly raccoon,
Hides his treats, sings to the moon.
With every bite, a clever jest,
In cloudy paths, they're all obsessed!

Murmurs of Jewel-Toned Whispers

In the garden, a giggle takes flight,
Jewel tones twirl, a comical sight.
Chasing the flavors, a flighty parade,
Laughter and juice in a sweet serenade.

A squirrel in shades, looking quite dapper,
Nibbling on treats, a fluffy chap's caper.
The berries conspire, so wild and so spry,
With each merry bounce, they make the stars sigh.

A bear with a grin, takes a taste with delight,
Accidentally rolling, what a comical plight!
The bushes all chuckle, the branches all sway,
As critters join in for this fruity ballet.

So here in this place, where fun never surrenders,
We'll sip on the joy, make laughter our vendors.
Each evening adorned with a riotous sound,
In whispers of color, pure bliss will abound.

Blooms of Night and Day

In the daylight, a dance of the bright,
Fruity adventures, oh, what a sight!
A rooster in shades, struts with a twist,
Chasing the shadows, none could resist.

At twilight, the giggles start to emerge,
Queer little critters begin their surge.
A hedgehog dons pearls, feeling so grand,
While bees buzz in laughter, an unexpected band.

With petals engaging in playful debate,
Each color a player, but none could relate.
They tumble together, in a chaotic spree,
In blooms of confusion, oh, how they flee!

As night covers all in a silvery shawl,
The mischief continues, none want to stall.
Under the moon's giggle, wild tales intertwine,
Where day meets the night in a zany design.

Singing the Harvest Tides

From fields full of cheer, the harvest arrives,
Fruits wearing hats as the laughter thrives.
With a skip and a hop, they roll to the shore,
In a sea of sweet jokes, they're begging for more!

A crab joins the fun, with a berry bouquet,
Trying to dance, in a sideways display.
While crows in the distance, perch above with flair,
Cracking up as they watch this chaotic affair.

The wind whistles tunes, winks to the sea,
A symphony silenced by berry jubilee.
In rhythm, they jive, frolic, and rhyme,
Catalysts of laughter, keeping perfect time.

With each tidal wave bringing fruit to the land,
Each harvest a comedy, so sweet and so grand.
Let’s toast to the joy, and the whimsy that tides,
In singing delight where hilarity abides.

Melancholy Tastes in Twilight's Embrace

As twilight descends with a sigh and a grin,
Fruits gather round, as silliness begins.
Wistful they ponder, their time on the vine,
But giggles escape like a bubbly red wine.

A raccoon in shades, holding court by a tree,
Regales us with tales of a fruit jubilee.
Alas! A mishap! A berry in flight,
Sightseeing raccoons in a sticky delight.

In shadows they mingle, concocting a scheme,
To savor the laughter, to sip on a dream.
As the stars twinkle on, wearing hats of bright glee,
They chuckle at twilight, so merry and free.

Thus twilight lingers, with a touch of sweet shame,
In the hearts of these fruits, we all know their names.
A party of colors, through laughter they race,
In melancholy moments, we find our true place.

Mosaic of Notes from the Ground

A purple stain on my shoe,
Hopping like frogs, what to do?
The laughter spills from the trees,
Tickling my thoughts like a tease.

Red delights rolling down hills,
Chasing with goofy, loud shrills.
The squirrels, they giggle and leap,
Whispering secrets, no need to peep.

Colors clash in a wild parade,
Each plump fruit has its own escapade.
Juggling flavors, a messy affair,
We dance like clowns without a care.

And when summer's sweet song is done,
There's hush, then we laugh and run.
Our festival loud, playful and bright,
A banquet of joy in the sunlight.

Garden Serenade in the Gentle Twilight

In the garden where shadows play,
Tomatoes tease, come out to sway.
Chortling blooms in the soft twilight,
Whispers of laughter take flight.

Fireflies twinkle like tiny stars,
Dodging my head like buzzing cars.
Each blossom giggles, shakes with cheer,
A melody of joy, so clear.

Join the rabbits, wild and spry,
Pants too short, oh my, oh my!
They trip on vines, dance in line,
While I chuckle at their design.

The veggies hum a silly tune,
As moonlight bathes the garden soon.
Beneath the glow, all dreams unfurl,
In this funny, whimsical world.

Vines of Gold Under the Moon

Golds and greens twist, a merry sight,
Bouncing about, what a delight!
The moon giggles, bright and bold,
With tales of mischief, stories told.

Whimsical squashes pull their pranks,
Turning twirls into silly flanks.
They shimmy and shake without a care,
While crickets join with a rhythmic flare.

Pumpkins roll and tumble down,
Making a mess of my old gown.
Laughter echoes through the sweet night,
As shadows dance in the moon's light.

A feast of chuckles, flavors collide,
In this riotous evening, we abide.
Celebrating all that is bright and funny,
In the garden where life is sweet as honey.

The Essence of Forgotten Fields

In fields where laughter has grown tall,
Wheat and daisies have much to sprawl.
A breezy kite flies overhead,
Heckling the cows that won't get fed.

The corn stalks whisper tales of fun,
Of antics played under the sun.
Each ear of corn, a wise old sage,
Recalling flings from a golden age.

Chasing the butterflies with a smile,
I stumble and trip, oh what a while!
Dirt on my nose, but who really cares?
We leap like frogs, untroubled by stares.

At dusk, the fields begin to sway,
Filled with happy sounds at play.
In this land where giggles blend,
Each turn and twist is just a friend.

Fruits Whispering in the Breeze

The cherries giggle in the trees,
While raspberries sway with such ease.
Blueberries bounce to a silly tune,
As strawberries blush under the moon.

Peaches tease with their fuzzy flair,
While lemons scrunch up, unaware.
Grapes rolling down the hillside steep,
Crackle with laughter, never sleep.

The apples chuckle, bright and round,
As plums make puns without a sound.
All join in a fruity parade,
Sprightly and sweet, delightfully made!

Oh, what fun in the orchard's play,
As nature's sweets bring joy each day.
With laughter spilling like sweet juice,
The breeze carries smiles, oh so profuse!

Echoes of Nature's Harvest

In orchards ripe, the laughter grows,
Peaches whisper as mischief flows.
Pineapples wear bright party hats,
While angry lemons scowl at cats.

Pastel melons slide with grace,
Dancing lightly, a fresh embrace.
Kiwi giggles, fuzzy and bold,
Witty tales of sweetness told.

Ripe figs hum a tuneful joke,
While mangoes tease with a little poke.
The harvest sings in fruity tone,
Echoes of joy, not meant to be lone.

With every bite, a chuckle sprouts,
Nature's bounty, what fun it's about!
So let the laughter fill the air,
Harvest merry, beyond compare!

Sweetness Carried by the Zephyr

The gentle breeze, it sings so sweet,
As fruit makes friends with dancing feet.
The limes roll over with a smile,
While pineapples strike a pose for a while.

Dancing citrus, with zesty cheer,
Popcorn berries join in near.
Hilarious grapes tumble and spin,
Joking about the juice within.

Watermelons burst into song,
As they all gawk at the cantaloupe throng.
Tart little cranberries start a jest,
Double-taking on the fruity fest.

Twinkling flavors float through the air,
Juicy punchlines for all to share.
In this breeze of giggles so fine,
Tasting laughter, oh how divine!

The Dance of Crimson Delights

Ripe raspberries whirl, oh so bright,
Swaying left, then they whirl right.
Cherries do the cha-cha with flair,
As strawberries spin without care.

Cranberries clasp hands in a row,
Bouncing merrily to and fro.
The blueberries slip with a grin,
Holding back laughs that burst from within.

In this fruity waltz, the joy expands,
As blackberries twirl with sprinkled hands.
Fruity cheers rise up high,
As the laughter dances through the sky.

Each step is a giggle, each twirl a tease,
Fruits frolicking free in the soft breeze.
The dance goes on till the day turns bright,
With a full fruit bowl, it feels just right!

Vines Weaving Tales Among the Boughs

In the garden, a squirrel plays,
With a berry hat, he prances and sways.
He tells of the fruit that fell from its vine,
And danced through the air—oh! What a fine line!

The rabbits all giggle, they hop and they twirl,
As grapevines twist softly, like ribbons that swirl.
A porcupine chuckles, with spines all aglow,
'You'll never catch me in a wild berry throw!'

Underneath leafy bows, a fox sings out loud,
'If I charm all the birds, I shall draw in the crowd!'
The leaves rustle back with a jovial cheer,
'Come join in the fun, we've got snacks over here!'

Through brambles and thorns, they all take a chance,
To juggle the fruits, then break out in dance.
With laughter like bubbles that float on the breeze,
A berry-filled circus, oh won't you come please?

Lush Melodies in Silent Woods

In the shade of the pines, where the giggles reside,
A hedgehog sings sweetly, with berries as pride.
The tunes are a blend of the twinkling sun,
While crickets add rhythm, oh aren’t we having fun?

A bushy-tailed rabbit hops up with a jig,
Waving her paws in a berry-stained gig.
'I’ll show you my dance,' she declares with a grin,
'In this lush frolic, the fun can’t begin!'

The owls on the branches hoot softly and wise,
As ponies trot by, all decked out in fries.
They're munching on grasses, but look! There they wade,
In a creek filled with laughter—what a wild parade!

Each berry a note in a chorus so bright,
In the woods where the buzz and the chirping unite.
With chuckles and glee, they dance in a swirl,
Come join in the mischief, let’s give it a twirl!

The Rainbow's Hidden Orchard

In the secret grove, where colors collide,
A gnomish old fellow takes pride in his stride.
With pockets of laughter, all filled to the brim,
He's the jolly protector, and joy's his sweet hymn.

The fruit sings in hues, cherries blush and giggle,
While lemons roll down, making everyone wiggle.
A grinning chihuahua guards this fruity loot,
With a berry-like crown and a snazzy green suit!

Grumpiest turtles clutch crusty old shells,
Trade puns for ripe peaches, oh how it compels!
With jokes in the air and confetti of fun,
They throw in a dance 'til the setting of sun.

A parade of delight, underneath leafy lanes,
They twirl on the grass, stirring up silly gains.
With each step they slip, a volley of cheer,
The orchard's alive—join the laughter right here!

Sweet Cascades of Nature's Laughter

By the brook where we gather, the chuckles abound,
In the air, sweet giggles form laughter profound.
Each splash from the water, a joke takes flight,
As frogs in their tuxedos leap left and then right.

A crow with a wink plays the jesting bard,
Dropping berries like cannonballs, oh how hard!
The turtles are laughing while floating with glee,
'Just bob along, friend! Come join our jamboree!'

The sun beams down bright, tickling each leaf,
While ladybugs tango, unbowed and belief.
With sparkles of fun uncontained in their eyes,
Nature's own revelers transform into spies!

So let’s gather the fruits, no frown to be found,
For joy reigns supreme, and it turns all around.
In laughter, we thrive, through each tickle and tease,
The joy of this moment, a sweet summer breeze!

Enchanted by the Wild Abundance

A creature danced with such a flair,
Its hat was made of fruity fare.
It tossed about the sweet delights,
As flavors soared to dizzy heights.

The squirrels laughed, the rabbits cheered,
As munchkins wiggled, none had feared.
With every toss, a giggle sprung,
A feast of joy, the song was sung.

And though the pie was gone, oh dear,
The laughter echoed far and near.
For in the wild, absurdity,
Is nature's surest comedy.

So skip along through fields so wide,
And let your silly spirit ride.
With every wink the day can lend,
A merry prankster, never end.

Nature's Whimsy on a Gentle Gale

A gust of laughter tickled leaves,
The daisies danced with sudden heaves.
A bouncing berry hit a tree,
And knocked the bird out of its spree.

The chipmunks snickered at the scene,
As marshmallow clouds bobbed and leaned.
A bear on unicycles rolled,
With summer's flavors to behold.

The breeze was stuffed with giggling treats,
Cheeky smiles in every sweep.
The trees waved back, a comical jest,
In nature’s game, we are all blessed.

So let your laughter fill the air,
With each ripe moment, joy to share.
In this enchanted, fragrant spin,
Who knows where the fun might begin?

Harmonies of Nature's Delights

A chorus rose from prickly vines,
With berries strumming silly lines.
The frogs croaked bass, the birds sang high,
As fruity giggles filled the sky.

The strawberries twirled with merry might,
While blueberries joined the wild delight.
A melting jam with giggly zings,
In every note, joy freely sings.

In fields where every color bursts,
The laughter flows and never thirsts.
With every flavor, each bright taste,
We dance through dreams, no moments waste.

So join the ruckus, don’t be shy,
For nature's tunes are passing by.
With harmonies of joy outpoured,
We celebrate, the fun restored!

Chasing Shadows of Flickering Fruits

A flash of pink went zipping past,
Was that a snack or shadows cast?
The peaches giggled in the shade,
While plums and cherries pranced and played.

A sneaky raccoon, paws on his chin,
Felt the thrill of the fruity din.
It darted left then straight and right,
With chuckles blaring, a silly sight.

The shadows danced with every leap,
As juicy treasures dared to creep.
In wild pursuits of fruity flair,
The fun was found in snares and air.

So twirl and tumble, chase the glee,
For every shadow’s just a spree.
And in the chase, the laughter spreads,
In nature’s dance, be light, be led.

The Sweetness of Wandering Spirits

In fields of laughter, they glide and sway,
Chasing shadows until the end of day.
With giggles that tickle the sun’s warm glow,
They paint the air with a vibrant show.

Juggling joy like a circus clown,
They flip and spin, never wearing a frown.
Whispers of mischief swirl in delight,
As they dance in circles, oh, what a sight!

Bees buzz along, intrigued by their play,
While insects join in for a wacky ballet.
Unearthed treasures from soft, squishy ground,
Such silly surprises are joyfully found.

So if you’re wandering, keep your eyes peeled,
For secret giggles are often revealed.
In the sweetness of spirit, we’ll surely find,
A world full of laughter, there’s no need to mind.

Coursing Through Berry-Stained Dreams

Puddles of color splat in the air,
A splash of whimsy with a dash of flair.
Dreams on the verge of a playful spree,
Whirling through whims like a circus marquee.

Chasing the stars in a berry-bright dance,
Where every silly slip is a second chance.
The giggles ripple like waves on a shore,
As laughter echoes, “Please, give me more!”

Straw hats tipped at impossible heights,
Floppy and floppy, they’re full of delights.
With whispers of fruit, they caper and bounce,
As friends find their rhythm, in mistakes they announce!

So wander through dreams, where the fun never ends,
In a berry-stained world, we’ll make new friends.
With laughter as ripe as the fruit on the vine,
Let’s dance through our dreams, it’s berry divine!

Driftwood Sentinels of Taste

On shores of flavor, driftwood stands tall,
Guardians of sweetness, they welcome us all.
With quirky stories, they whisper to the sand,
Inventive and tasty, they humorously stand.

The waves tickle toes, while snacks drift past,
Forgotten delights are gathered so fast.
Crackling confessions from old wooden beams,
Bring laughter and joy on our snack-laden dreams.

A picnic explodes with surprises galore,
Each morsel enchanting, akin to folklore.
We nibble and chuckle beneath sunny skies,
Savoring moments as laughter complies.

So raise up your cups to driftwood that knows,
The way to a meal where the fun freely flows.
In the crunch of the season, no moment's a waste,
With serendipity leading to marvelous taste!

The Taste of Forgotten Summers

In corners of memories, summers do gleam,
Each taste is a story, a flickering dream.
With popsicle smiles and sun-soaked delight,
The laughter lingers, it dances at night.

Picnic tables, dressed up for a feast,
With slip-ups and spills, our joy's been released.
Splatters of flavor like watercolor skies,
Silly surprises that tickle our eyes.

Sailing the winds as the day drifts away,
The sun dips down, giving shadow its play.
Finding delight in the simplest things,
Like cookies with sprinkles and ridiculous swings.

So let's spin our tales of forgotten delight,
With laughter and flavors that shine through the night.
The taste of our summers, forever they'll claim,
A mix of sweet whispers in life's bustling game.

www.ingramcontent.com/pod-product-compliance
Lightning Source LLC
Chambersburg PA
CBHW060143230426
43661CB00003B/547
9781805864141